Providence Sonnets 1-33, The Persecutions

Jon Woodson

Wild Pineapple Press

Providence, Rhode Island

Inspired by Umberto Crenca's "Divine Providence" series of Providence, Rhode Island street scenes "Providence Sonnets, 1-33, The Persecutions" venture beyond literal descriptions (ekphrasis). The sonnets shuffle history, anecdote, art, literature, and philosophy, like a pack of Tarot cards laid out to depict the past, present, and future in a kaleidoscope of simultaneous images and voices.

1.
John Cotton's providence fructifies down

and move no more so that they plainly see

       a providence of God

The placing of a people in this or that country

predicts a storm at 4:00 p.m. and kwee kwee

even now the ships ride at anchor

flying over seas and rocks, and all hindrances

but he cannot hope there is anything for him

as he carried a burning brand toward the ships

Was their ever such a bulwark? Such towers?

improvised, wooden world, peopled by soldiers

       and their captured women.

the ospreys slide along with the darkening clouds

just so the fleshy sibyl on local cable

the poet becomes the heroic interrogator

       of America's ideals

the page—a clutch of wild grapes ripening

2.
Spiritual artillery and weapons are proper

Only don't look like you are in a hurry,

I give you workers without organs of human dignity

I don't want means any more than I want meanings

labour-time is a condition of commodification

burned by order of Parliament

persecution by fragmentation of the socially

      necessary body

looking down I want choruses of order

soul-rape determines the bus schedule and the weather

tolerate the wolf and the thief will tender

living in mere skeletons, shadows and carcasses,

O one warfare supernaturally

my supporters the back and forth of tennis balls

Therefore take heed how you proceed against me

3.

"I have looked upon all that the universe
 has to hold of horror: peaceful coexistence
between individuals of different social
classes sweep clean the path for a new culture
Then the horrible warning upon my soul sped
the 'new man', who arises out of the victorious
revolution just as Darwin discovered
the law of evolution in organic nature,
so Marx discovered the law of evolution
in human history, where Thermidorian
reaction is now reaching its climax
Naked man in the stark desert exaggerates
he is to report in his secret autobiography
at least a peeping chick will begin to break forth

4.

Like as not to unknown constellations

the lantern glows on China clippers and packets

spread along the wicked waterfront

moved heaven into the waters of Providence

trading in bodies, rum, and opium

until steam replaced manpower, the shoreline

lined with warehouses, wharves, and piers

and factories rose along the byways

I'd dressed in all the clothing I had brought

and went down and sat near the road

the houses were looking at me with

      their sad-eyed windows

I began to paint their portrait

934 vessels left for African ports

bringing in 106,000 persons with wandering stars

5.

With your broom on the walk

        you look so married

Do you know that the wages of sin is death?

we will miss the dynamic process

        by which culture is created

these narratives of transition

        expect the same ending

each new thing has formed 266 new signs

I arrange a curt reply to a white city

the seven phases of my seven forms

sealed me again in my voices, the willow wind

Lovecraft describing Poe on Benefit Street

but there's little subtlety in this performance

There's no oral stories that say

        we crossed a bridge or anything else

but the apocalyptic feel is intensified

a field of experience which is external to us,

requires normality, sanity, everydayness

6.

The riot of roofers was named Bobby:

I implored the Bobby in charge

       to look at my garage—

the roof had been done wrongly and now ants

were at the boards and since they were already

working just down the street what was the chance?

Fragmentary thought brings pain unforeseen—

war from nations, but you know

       who moved your arm.

Out of this non-duality emerges the entire

world of roofs, intersections of space-time,

rampant angles not separate or separable.

There were materials left over and half a day

that I could have for a good price as long

as I didn't care about the color of the shingles.

Our things in our hands must be equals, Comrades.

The world of people and things is the world.

7.

DO NOT ENTER

And even the lone surviving kamikaze pilot
has to be put away and a semblance of oeuvre
strutted in support of the here and now
concrete umbrellas, dogs that run along
counting back from one hundred the oculomotor
odiums accorded property lines in spray paint
exhaustion can you paint in a bath house?
Darger put it all down wrong, Merkin quoted
both too social, insulting, inappropriate, hobnob.
Hoicks. Cement overcoats implied by big hats,
and naked women under flags just in shoes,
no justice unless you are laughing through hoist
Can't get out of Providence, improvident—
two-timing your class, murder for fun, Felix?

8.

Walking to China, the Darien Gap

That the frenziedness of technology

may entrench itself in experience of loss

everywhere to such an extent that someday,

a tentative coming-to-truth of pass

employs a long sonnet influenced by Hopkins

a testimony of the life of a modern man

but sometimes he mangles the syntax

       to make a sound

far from it—a philosophy of orgasm

born in in Rhode Island in 1934

to breathe, trochee, unstress, amendment

slapped awake in Tulsa by a sandwich

nostalgia is a warm coast, a coat or

now you won't ever do it before what?

traveling back in time to the Red Bridge

9.

Sky full of tools, windows water backward waves
those who aren't addicted to reason and meaning
cruel little captains beside themselves with wives
upright wall of hill-brow furrowed with tunnels
humans darkened out of lawlessness glances
under their stone names the generations leaning
indicators of steeples weathering advances
Hence she desires to be and belongs among the fish
Oral and Ariel throwing parties on Benefit Street
There was a kind of abjectness about the way
        things were made.
Head full of Portuguese strumming
        and thoughts in runnels
that which shines forth most purely profited
held in contempt and arranged like fallen leaves
purling anew our look of arms of water and masts

10.

Machinization of our own views on ourselves:

green light beams pulsating with the rhythm

      of the heartbeats of passersby,

And she was already late for work.

the ladder on its side, the receding perspective

      of worn tools

punch cards, scrolls of paper, or a mesh

      of wires on a wall.

filaments, surfaces corroded by chemical rain

zones where we as humans could still resist such

(I am what I think you think I am).

tarantulas are pretty harmless and rarely

      bite humans.

many media art projects intentionally

      confuse their audiences.

and shatter on the floor like glass

What does being an "agent" capable

      of producing change involve?

(automata, dolls, avatars, body doubles)

Scared of the meteor? if I earn your forgiveness

a "margin of error" is needed to correct

      behavior in real time,

11.

Dan came into the room where the sash was lifted

and saw the culprit with his shoes in hand.

After that he put stops on the windows

      to hinder thieves.

After Julie ran off with a photographer

      and Dan declined,

the apartment was rented by a prospective couple.

They decorated in all the new shades—

      forest green, burgundy, browns

and brought in angled futuristic furniture.

After the wedding all of the boxes

      the presents came in

were inventoried in an empty stack

      outside the back door.

in the air strange screams of death

We ran to see what dire combustion

      and confused entrance

new hatched to the woeful bride had

      broken out below

The predictable felons had found no hindrance

and crept and carried off the very meaning of the vow.

12.

Ocean State Tackle

We shut our eyes and dissolve into darkness.

and the braid has no stretch so the bite can

      be felt easily

He drifts in form, structure, music, image movement,

but in all of that drifting, he is most true

      to himself, I think.

Monks turned to reusing older parchments

      when supplies at the monastery ran scarce.

A girl alive with his hooks through her lips;

Trying to relate quantum mechanics

      to consciousness is tough.

All his life was practice, whether he was sitting

      in meditation, writing, teaching, or sleeping.

And then come the wrecked angels and set snares,

And bait them with light hopes and heavy dreams,

They offer the bait in a more visible position

      than hooks or rigs

yet their cultural DNA exists in our culture today

Why did art bear the modest name techne?

I think dream theory can help us here.

      You understand.

13.

Shall I compare you to Utrillo's lane?

La Rue Norvins à Montmartre, oil on board, c. 1910

I have no host in battle him to prove,

Valadon, who became a model after a

      fall from a trapeze

ended her chosen career as a circus acrobat,

With no training beyond what his mother taught him,

he drew and painted what he saw in Montmartre.

No city walls are left for him to gain,

Rendered in thickly troweled paint,

the artist portrayed the winding streets and alleyways

a painter called Quiet, a solitary like himself,

with whom he painted in the streets

the despairing nakedness of certain forgotten

      corners of the suburbs.

14.

Rushing and careless I looked again for the word

from another art: what poem can

      come from the meat market?

We want that which shines forth purely

Some colorful bird that calls down from a branch—

sustains your life in the unsmiling climate.

the sacrifices made to pacify the hungers.

"One Cent, Five Cent, Ten Cent, Dollar"

dala dala dala dala

The awning is red to allay your doubts.

You without imagination can look up

      and see the burnt offerings,

these cuts of meat are promises, this hot food

to shine forth again from strings or from words.

Is it ekphanestaton that got away like a parrot?

that named one art calling forth a response

15.

The Purchase

We bought our bungalow unseen, secondhand, at agent,

and were haply desperate when we closed: so parallel

to Pettaquamscutt Rock. I've been there, have you and yours?

Choked in by shrubbery and thick undergrowth hiking

behind Devine that time, disgusted. Pathfinder

with not a hair out of place. Out of place.

        Can only narrowly see.

Take me to the top I insisted. We go up to Tower Hill.

Right at the point where you can see across land

        and water to Newport

there was a cairn and a large rock. "This is where

        they sighted in the Purchase,"

I speculated. Later I gave a lecture

        and offered up my charge.

That same week I was approached by La Farge

and grimly told, never speak of this again.

        I got out my surveys

to work out why I'd be savaged. It was clear

        that my debate

would queer the whole deal for his estate.

16.

Capitalism is an immense and complex
            organisation of time,
where the weeds grow up in the cracks
because they are sustained though unwanted
and expand contrary to interpretations
a teleological living being like capital
beyond the swing of the gate or step of foot
either spreading weblike or reaching vinelike
for sustenance commodified here
there is bitterness in their minds
the weed comes unbidden and is the future
turning into rapture with pink excrescences
an idea of protonema finding its way to xylem
Proudhoun a providence, money not clock
as a world system having no place or time

17.

No wish to speak among the savages

Let it be said that things are in my way,

the gates opened to let out the cars

inconsiderately left blocking the walk

so that I can either close them or die there

though I could go inside and live in that house

these are the sharp things that leave me open

to dangerous questions of my role here

in a world where the owner might return

and find me waiting for an apology

or might find me reading a handbook within

or even the inspirational book left

on the bedside table the Holy Ghost had shook

as though it were another language pulled away

18.

William Burroughs, Bobby Short and
                Krazy Kat are missing
and the emotionally peculiar descriptions
                of their fallen bodies:
 Euryalus, Lausus, Pallas, and Camilla.
With exuberant polyptoton Dido
picks up this double sense in her curse
with the Georgian doorway and
                interior paneling
dictated by the timely progress of taste
"I'se be catchin' ma feets nah, Boss."
John Cotton, a Visible Saint among
                the reformed church
the change from stones to shells woke me
out of this jurisdiction, charged with folly
giving the deep cellar a street
                frontage with a door
"That awful door in Benefit Street
                which I had left ajar."
the banks of eternity will pay for all

19.

"Adrift in a sea of permissiveness,

      they have little to rebel against."

it's me that is ephemeral; only I am in doubt

the Quakers a lazy violent lot

the great sidereal tracks are lighted up

today I have completely understood their source

one moon appears in all bodies of water

what is the point of two intentions in one passage?

the treasure had been hidden in someone's mind

anger o anger who is behind me?

why do investors believe they can do

      better than the market?

it is not the light it is the eye that brings

      the city to life

coming back led by leviathans gamboling

he gets older and older the mind his game

and I subdue the world in a black mirror

20.

John Cotton's providence fructifies down

the page—a clutch of wild grapes ripening

and move no more so that they plainly see

a providence of God

the poet becomes the heroic interrogator

of America's ideals

The placing of a people in this or that country

just so the fleshy sibyl on local cable

predicts a storm at 4:00 p.m. and kwee kwee

the ospreys slide along with the darkening clouds

even now the ships ride at anchor

improvised, wooden world, peopled by soldiers

and their captured women.

flying over seas and rocks, and all hindrances

Was their ever such a bulwark? Such towers?

but he cannot hope there is anything for him

as he carried a burning brand toward the ships

21.

With your broom on the walk you look so married

we will miss the dynamic process by

        which culture is created

each new thing has formed 266 new signs

the seven phases of my seven forms

Lovecraft describing Poe on Benefit Street

There's no oral stories that say we crossed

        a bridge or anything else

a field of experience which is external to us,

traveling back in time to the Red Bridge

nostalgia is a warm coast, a coat or

to breathe, trochee, unstress, amendment

far from it—a philosophy of orgasm

a testimony of the life of a modern man

a tentative coming-to-truth of pass

may entrench itself in experience of loss

22.

Do you know that the wages of sin is death?

these narratives of transition

      expect the same ending

I arrange a curt reply to a white city

sealed me again in my voices, the willow wind

but there's little subtlety in this performance

but the apocalyptic feel is intensified

requires normality, sanity, everydayness

that the frenziedness of technology

everywhere to such an extent that someday,

employs a long sonnet influenced by Hopkins

but sometimes he mangles the syntax

      to make a sound

born in in Rhode Island in 1934

slapped awake in Tulsa by a sandwich

now you won't ever do it before what?

23.

The shadow runs from punishment

"whoosh-WHOOM!" sighs the hypotenuse across

You respond to the least wind.

impenetrable ciphers for indifferent eyes

a collection of capital cities made out of toothpicks

think of it as graffiti with throughput

the world's your quahog

and we were fooled into believing in life again

farms divide the land tilled and tilled again

the children who had never been any

       place but Providence

my book gone up in flames

weak souls are flying scattered for shelter

the water of the Seekonk flows by

reconstruct the puzzle in your own mind

24.

The narrator searches for the City of Immortals

the city projected on the land, fragmented,

erases the bodies, leaving the living without organs.

There will never be new toilets by Lovecraft,

there will never be new bath houses by Poe.

Hygiene thus has life cycles different from science,

many people are making journeys

in search of excretion, leaving home

in order to interweave their necessities

as defined by margins and the names of rivers.

Pointless arrows, locked doors, time codes,

determine when the ground opens

for explanation. I remember my own panic

but I scratched my mind to pieces for peace

25.

Single Unit Portable Toilet at the Dexter Training Ground

—I am not pathologically attracted to this topic:

even Freud couldn't find a public toilet in New York in 1909.

I was playing bocce at the Dexter Training Ground,

when I experienced acute discomfort.

When I found the portable toilet, it was repulsive.

It was a hot day, and the tank had collected for weeks.

The next time I played bocce, the porta-potty was gone.

I observed the homeless people gathered under trees.

I watched the ball game regularly played.

I wondered about the children fed there by the city.

I pondered the irony of an enclosure for the comfort of dogs.

Providence has the public sanitation of a third world country.

It is intolerable that the taboo nature of the topic

lets politicians avoid a crisis that sows misery and sickness.

26.

We will miss the dynamic process by which

      culture is created

each new thing has formed 266 new signs

the seven phases of my seven forms

I wondered about the children fed there by the city.

It was a hot day, and the tank had collected for weeks.

even Freud couldn't find a public toilet

      in New York in 1909.

where the weeds grow up in the cracks

because they are sustained though unwanted

and expand contrary to interpretations

capitalism is an immense and complex

      organisation of time,

when I experienced acute discomfort.

I observed the homeless people gathered under trees.

Providence has the public sanitation

      of a third world country

I arrange a curt reply to a white city

these narratives of transition expect the same ending

27.

I arrange a curt reply to a white city

these narratives of transition expect

      the same ending

requires normality, sanity, everydayness

It was a hot day, and the tank had collected for weeks.

we will miss the dynamic process by which

      culture is created

where the weeds grow up in the cracks

I wondered about the children fed there by the city.

because they are sustained though unwanted

Our things in our hands must be equals, Comrades.

and expand contrary to interpretations

capitalism is an immense and complex

      organisation of time,

when I experienced acute discomfort.

I observed the homeless people gathered under trees.

at the peril of the entire body politic.

Can't we see better with the lights on?

28.

But sometimes he mangles the syntax to make a sound

and we were fooled into believing in life again

anger o anger who is behind me?

these are the sharp things that leave me open

as a world system having no place or time

Rendered in thickly troweled paint,

And then come the wrecked angels and set snares,

in the air strange screams of death

(I am what I think you think I am).

a testimony of the life of a modern man

two-timing your class, murder for fun, Felix?

I am come in my broken coach

whole forests on my shoulders

at this point the discoverer begins to have visions

29.

Rushing and careless I looked again for the word

that named one art calling forth a response

from another art: what poem can come

      from the meat market?

Is it ekphanestaton that got away like a parrot?

We want that which shines forth purely

to shine forth again from strings or from words.

Some colorful bird that calls down from a branch—

these cuts of meat are promises, this hot food

sustains your life in the unsmiling climate.

You without imagination can look up

      and see the burnt offerings,

the sacrifices made to pacify the hungers.

The awning is red to allay your doubts.

"One Cent, Five Cent, Ten Cent, Dollar"

dala dala dala dala dala

30.

Lack and slot and slay and lost and cheer,

chairs before the door, care and sorbet break

demand the one thing readied cornucopia

stalled coinage pacified on your knees peace

path protected by hope, foolishness, totality

knock and the beliefs fly up like sparrows

where is your mind now? sit and search for yourself

in the abyss. provide, provision, progeny

one by one like the fist at the door. don't

come in here unprepared. we are all hunted,

hindered, making it up, hiding handsomely

bring a rhyme to teach the head to bow wow,

cast out the knotty, reign in the singular

go to the streets enraptured, angelic

31.

"I have looked upon all that the universe

between individuals of different social

Then the horrible warning upon my soul sped

revolution just as Darwin discovered

so Marx discovered the law of evolution

reaction is now reaching its climax

he is to report in his secret autobiography

at least a peeping chick will begin to break forth

Naked man in the stark desert exaggerates

in human history, where Thermidorian

the law of evolution in organic nature,

the 'new man', who arises out of the victorious

classes sweep clean the path for a new culture

has to hold of horror: peaceful coexistence

32.

Spiritual artillery and weapons are proper

I give you workers without organs of human dignity

labour-time is a condition of commodification

persecution by fragmentation of the socially

       necessary body

soul-rape determines the bus schedule and the weather

living in mere skeletons, shadows and carcasses,

my supporters the back and forth of tennis balls

Therefore take heed how you proceed against me

O one warfare supernaturally

tolerate the wolf and the thief will tender

looking down I want choruses of order

burned by order of Parliament

I don't want means any more than I want meanings

Only don't look like you are in a hurry,

33.

When you were not reading the forbidden books

on warm days you took the guitar into the yard

your fingers traced the black afflictions

the rental was tucked behind the landlord's:

they screamed all day to mark the genocide

when the cousin collapsed at the door you caught her

you had not known that the sick woman never left

when she came out one day into the sunlight

you had been sitting under her window

playing all those months as though alone

she was all that time on her sickbed

daily your songs came in at the window

keeping her company taking her along

then she thanked you for her recovery

www.ingramcontent.com/pod-product-compliance
Lightning Source LLC
Chambersburg PA
CBHW071241140726
47996CB00007B/2703